United States Presidents

George W. Bush

Patrick Ryan
ABDO Publishing Company

visit us at
www.abdopub.com

Published by Abdo Publishing Company, 4940 Viking Drive, Edina, Minnesota 55435.
Copyright © 2001 by Abdo Consulting Group, Inc. International copyrights reserved in all
countries. No part of this book may be reproduced in any form without written permission
from the publisher.

Printed in the United States.

Photo Credits: AP/Wide World, Corbis

Contributing Editors: Bob Italia, Tamara L. Britton, Kate A. Furlong, Christine Fournier
Art Direction: Neil Klinepier

Library of Congress Cataloging-in-Publication Data

Ryan, Patrick, 1948-
   George W. Bush / Patrick Ryan.
      p. cm. -- (United States presidents)
   ISBN 1-57765-302-5
    1. Bush, George W. (George Walker), 1946---Juvenile literature. 2.
Governors--Texas--Biography--Juvenile literature. 3. Presidential candidates--
United States--Biography--Juvenile literature. 4. Children of presidents--United
States--Biography--Juvenile literature. 5. Texas--Politics and
government--1951---Juvenile literature. 6. Presidents--United
States--Election--2000--Juvenile literature. [1. Bush, George W. (George Walker), 1946-
2. Governors. 3. Presidential candidates.] I. Title. II. United States presidents (Edina,
Minn.)

F391.4.B87 R93 2001
976.4'063'092--dc21
[B]
                                                  00-050431

Contents

George W. Bush

*I*n 2000, Americans elected George W. Bush the forty-third president of the United States. He won one of the closest elections in U.S. history.

Bush grew up in Texas. Then he moved to the east coast to attend high school and college. After graduating, Bush served in the Texas Air National Guard. Then he attended Harvard Business School.

After Harvard, Bush had many jobs. He worked in the oil **industry**. Then he was co-owner of the Texas Rangers baseball team. He also worked on his father's presidential campaign.

In 1994, Texans elected Bush as governor. Governor Bush improved education, cut taxes, and **reformed** the **welfare** system. He was re-elected in 1998.

Republicans nominated Bush for president in 2000. He ran against Vice President Al Gore. Both candidates campaigned hard. It was a long, close race. After the election, it took over a month to figure out who had won.

George W. Bush

George W. Bush (1946-)
Forty-third President

BORN:	July 6, 1946
PLACE OF BIRTH:	New Haven, Connecticut
ANCESTRY:	English
FATHER:	George Herbert Walker Bush (1924-)
MOTHER:	Barbara Pierce Bush (1925-)
WIFE:	Laura Welch (1946-)
CHILDREN:	Twin daughters
EDUCATION:	Phillips Academy
	Yale University, B.A.
	Harvard Business School, M.B.A.
RELIGION:	Methodist
OCCUPATION:	Businessman
MILITARY SERVICE:	Second lieutenant, Texas Air National Guard
POLITICAL PARTY:	Republican

OFFICES HELD:	Governor of Texas
AGE AT INAUGURATION:	54
YEARS SERVED:	2001-
VICE PRESIDENT:	Dick Cheney

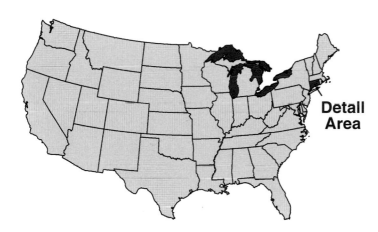

Detail
Area

Birthplace of George W. Bush

Young George

*G*eorge Walker Bush was born in New Haven, Connecticut, on July 6, 1946. He was the first child of George and Barbara Bush. The Bushes went on to have five more children named Robin, Jeb, Neil, Marvin, and Dorothy.

In 1948, George's family moved to Odessa, Texas. There, his father took a job at an oil company. In 1949, his father's job moved the family to California. But in 1950, the Bushes moved back to Texas for good.

The Bush family settled into a little blue house in Midland. George made friends with children in his neighborhood. They liked to ride their bikes and play baseball.

George attended Sam Houston Elementary School. One day in 1953, George saw his parents' car pull into the school parking lot. George ran out to meet them. He quickly realized his parents were upset. They told George his little sister Robin had died of **cancer**.

Robin's death saddened George for a long time. His parents were sad, too. George tried to cheer them up by telling jokes and playing games.

The Bush family in 1948 (from left to right): mother Barbara, George W., father George, and grandparents Dorothy and Prescott

School Days

*D*uring this time, George's father was spending much time in Houston, Texas. Houston was near the Gulf of Mexico, where his oil wells were. So in 1959, the Bushes moved to a new house in Houston.

George did well in school. In junior high, he played quarterback on the football team. He was also elected class president.

George's parents wanted him to have the best education possible. So in 1961, they sent him to Phillips Academy in Andover, Massachusetts.

At Andover, George missed his family. He struggled with his lessons. He feared he might flunk out of school.

But George decided to do his best. He stayed up late studying. He made many new friends. He played on the baseball and football teams. He was also on the cheerleading squad.

George graduated from Andover in 1964. That summer, he returned to Texas. George helped his father campaign for the U.S. **Senate**. His father lost the election. But George gained valuable experience in politics.

That fall, George entered Yale University. At Yale, he played baseball and rugby. He joined a **fraternity** and was elected its president.

When George graduated in 1968, America was fighting the **Vietnam War**. George supported the government's decision to fight. So he joined the Texas Air National Guard.

George W. Bush was Andover's head cheerleader in 1964.

Flight School

*I*n July 1968, Bush left for Lackland Air Base in San Antonio, Texas. There, he went through basic training.

That November, he began flight training at Moody Air Force Base in Valdosta, Georgia. He started training on T-41 airplanes. Then he moved up to a more powerful plane called the T-38. Training was hard. Many people dropped out.

Bush earned his National Guard wings in December 1969. His father came to the **ceremony** and pinned on his wings. He was now a **second lieutenant**.

Soon, he left for his first assignment at Ellington Air Force Base in Houston. There, he learned to fly the F-102 fighter plane. His job with the National Guard was to protect the American coasts.

In 1970, Bush helped his father campaign for a seat on the U.S. **Senate**. They traveled around Texas and gave speeches. But Bush's father lost the election.

That summer, Bush finished his flight training. But on the weekends, he still flew for the National Guard.

After graduation, Bush had several jobs. First, he worked as an office assistant at an agricultural company. Next, he worked on a U.S. **Senate** campaign in Alabama. Then, he got a job working with poor children in Houston.

In 1973, Bush left for Harvard Business School in Cambridge, Massachusetts.

George W. Bush as a pilot in the Texas Air National Guard

The Making of the Forty-third United States President

1946
Born July 6 in New Haven, Connecticut

1948
Family moves to Odessa, Texas

1949
Family moves to California

1950
Family moves to Midland, Texas

1964
Graduates from Andover; works on father's Senate campaign; enters Yale University

1968
Graduates from Yale; joins Texas Air National Guard

1969
Earns National Guard pilot's wings

1970
Works on father's Senate campaign

1978
Runs for Congress, loses

1981
Daughters Jenna and Barbara born; changes company name to Bush Exploration

1984
Spectrum 7 buys Bush Exploration

1986
Harken Energy buys Spectrum 7

George W. Bush

"I was not elected to serve one party, but to serve one nation."

➡ **1953** ➡ **1959** ➡ **1961**

1953
Sister Robin dies

1959
Family moves to Houston, Texas

1961
Enters Phillips Academy in Andover, Massachusetts

Historic Events during Bush's Lifetime

Britain grants independence to India

U.S. astronaut Neil Armstrong is the first person to walk on the moon

U.S. president Richard Nixon resigns

➡ **1973** ➡ **1975** ➡ **1977**

1973
Enters Harvard Business School

1975
Graduates from Harvard; returns to Midland, Texas

1977
Starts Arbusto Energy; marries Laura Welch

➡ **1988** ➡ **1989** ➡ **1994** ➡ **1998** ➡

1988
Works on father's presidential campaign

1989
Joins investment group that buys Texas Rangers

1994
Elected governor of Texas

1998
Re-elected governor

2000
Elected president

Landman & Politician

*I*n 1975, Bush graduated from Harvard Business School. He wanted to work in the oil business. So he returned to his childhood home of Midland, Texas.

Bush's first job was as a landman. He looked up land **leases** at the **county** courthouse. The leases showed him who owned what land. If Bush thought a piece of land had oil in it, he called the owner. Then he asked if he could drill for oil on the land.

At first, Bush was unsuccessful. The holes he drilled had little or no oil. But soon he found a good piece of land. It had plenty of oil.

In 1977, Bush started his own oil company. He called it Arbusto Energy. But then Bush put his Arbusto plans on hold. He decided to campaign for **Congress** instead.

During this time, Bush met Laura Welch. She was a school librarian. On November 5, 1977, George and Laura got married.

Laura helped her husband campaign for **Congress**. Bush ran against Kent Hance. Hance claimed Bush was not a true Texan. Hance reminded voters that Bush had been born and educated outside of Texas. Texans disliked this. In 1978, Bush lost the election.

George W. Bush and his wife, Laura, campaign for Congress.

Businessman

*A*fter the election, Bush returned to Arbusto Energy. At first, the company did well. But oil prices quickly dropped. Bush had to raise money from **investors** to keep his business running.

At home, Bush's family was growing. In 1981, the Bushes had twin girls. They named the babies Jenna and Barbara.

Later that year, Bush changed the name of his company to Bush Exploration. He continued to raise money for the company. But the oil **industry** was falling apart. And Bush Exploration was losing money.

In 1984, a company called Spectrum 7 bought Bush Exploration. Bush became a partner at Spectrum 7. But the oil industry worsened. Spectrum 7 was nearly broke.

Bush knew Spectrum 7 needed help. So in 1986, he arranged a deal with Harken Energy. It agreed to buy Spectrum 7. Bush took a job at Harken as a **consultant**. And he served on the **board of directors**.

Shortly after the Harken deal, Bush turned 40 years old. On his birthday, he decided to make a change in his life. He stopped drinking **alcohol**. This helped him become a better husband, father, and businessman.

In 1988, Bush's father ran for president. Bush worked on the campaign. He made sure campaign workers were loyal to his father. He also gave speeches across the country. Bush's father easily won the election.

George W. Bush poses with his newborn daughters in 1981.

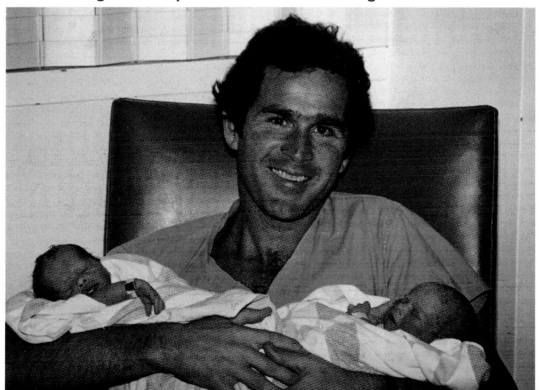

The Texas Rangers

*I*n 1988, Bill DeWitt Jr. called Bush. DeWitt was a friend of Bush's from Spectrum 7. He said the Texas Rangers baseball team was for sale.

The Rangers's owner, Eddie Chiles, was a Bush family friend. So DeWitt wanted Bush to bargain with Chiles. DeWitt also wanted Bush to join the group of **investors** that would buy the team.

Baseball commissioner Peter Ueberroth wanted local investors to buy the Rangers. So Bush brought several Texans into the investment group. In 1989, they bought the team.

Bush was the managing general partner. He acted as the investors' spokesman. Day-to-day operation of the team was handled by general manager Tom Grieve.

Soon Bush began working to build a new baseball stadium. But Texans did not want a new stadium. They said spending tax money on a stadium was **corporate welfare**.

But Bush said the project would be good for the state. He said it would bring many new jobs to Texas. Voters believed him. In 1991, Texans voted in favor of a new stadium.

Bush was proud of his accomplishments. He wanted to continue to help Texans. In 1993, he decided to run for governor.

George W. Bush in 1989, shortly after he became a co-owner of the Texas Rangers

Governor Bush

*B*ush ran against Texas governor Ann Richards. The campaign was hard. Richards was a popular governor. But Bush focused on what he thought was best for Texas. He wanted to lower crime rates, increase spending on education, and **reform** the **welfare** system.

Soon Richards realized Bush was pulling ahead in the race. So she began to attack Bush personally. She said mean things about him and his family.

Texans disliked Richards's attacks. But they liked what Bush had to say. Bush won the election in 1994.

As governor, Bush worked to return control of schools to local districts. He reduced the number of people in the welfare system. He supported bills that made punishment for **juvenile** criminals more strict. He also reduced property taxes.

Bush ran for re-election in 1998. This time he ran against Garry Mauro. Mauro had worked in Texas politics for many years.

But the people liked Bush. He had kept many of his campaign promises during his first term. He told Texans that he would continue to focus on education and **literacy**. He won the election in a landslide.

Governor Bush reads to students in Round Rock, Texas, in 1999. While at the school, Bush signed a law to improve education in Texas.

The Seven "Hats" of the U.S. President

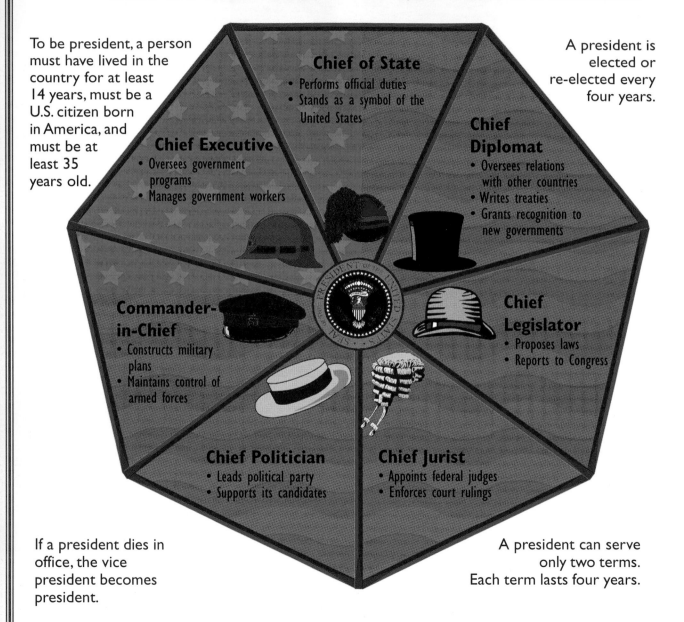

To be president, a person must have lived in the country for at least 14 years, must be a U.S. citizen born in America, and must be at least 35 years old.

A president is elected or re-elected every four years.

Chief of State
- Performs official duties
- Stands as a symbol of the United States

Chief Executive
- Oversees government programs
- Manages government workers

Chief Diplomat
- Oversees relations with other countries
- Writes treaties
- Grants recognition to new governments

Commander-in-Chief
- Constructs military plans
- Maintains control of armed forces

Chief Legislator
- Proposes laws
- Reports to Congress

Chief Politician
- Leads political party
- Supports its candidates

Chief Jurist
- Appoints federal judges
- Enforces court rulings

If a president dies in office, the vice president becomes president.

A president can serve only two terms. Each term lasts four years.

As president, George W. Bush has seven jobs.

The Three Branches of the U.S. Government

Congress is in the Capitol Building in Washington, D.C. It can pass laws and stop the president's veto. Congress can also change the Constitution to stop the president's plans or Supreme Court rulings.

The president lives in the White House in Washington, D.C. He or she can stop (veto) laws passed by Congress, and propose new laws. The president can also choose Supreme Court judges.

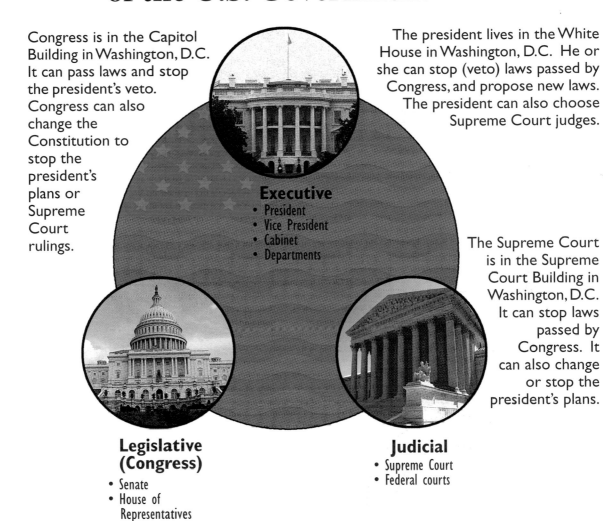

Executive
- President
- Vice President
- Cabinet
- Departments

The Supreme Court is in the Supreme Court Building in Washington, D.C. It can stop laws passed by Congress. It can also change or stop the president's plans.

Legislative (Congress)
- Senate
- House of Representatives

Judicial
- Supreme Court
- Federal courts

The U.S. Constitution formed three government branches. Each branch has power over the others. So no single group or person can control the country. The Constitution calls this "separation of powers."

Election 2000

*M*any **Republicans** liked Governor Bush's work in Texas. So in August 2000, the Republican party chose Bush as its candidate for president. Bush ran against Vice President Al Gore.

Bush traveled across the country during the campaign. He promised to **reform** education, cut taxes, and improve **Social Security**.

Americans voted on November 7, 2000. The candidate who received 270 **electoral votes** would win the election. At the end of the night, neither candidate had enough electoral votes to win.

Whoever won Florida's electoral votes would win the race. But Florida's election remained too close to call. Bush and Gore waited to hear who would get the state's 25 electoral votes.

On November 8, Bush won in Florida. But he beat Gore by only a few hundred votes. Florida law says if an election is that close, the **ballots** must be recounted. After the recount, Bush was still the winner.

Electoral Votes, 2000

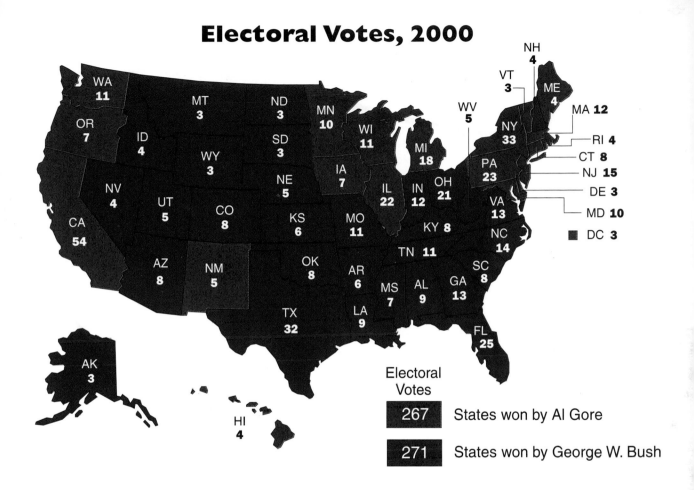

	Electoral Votes	
	267	States won by Al Gore
	271	States won by George W. Bush

Each state has electoral votes equal to the number of representatives it has in Congress. The state's population determines its number of representatives. States with large populations get more electoral votes.

When a candidate wins a state's popular vote, he or she wins its electoral votes. Al Gore won more popular votes than George W. Bush. But Bush won more electoral votes. So Bush won the 2000 election.

Gore thought there was a mistake. He felt that voting machines had not counted some of the votes. He wanted election workers to recount the **ballots** by hand in four **counties**. Florida's government permitted the hand recounts.

But Bush felt that the first two vote counts had been fair. He thought Gore's idea of hand counting ballots in only four counties was illegal. So Bush filed lawsuits in state and federal courts.

Bush lost his lawsuits. So he **appealed** to the U.S. **Supreme Court**. It made its final decision on December 12, 2000. It stopped all hand recounts in Florida. So Gore did not have enough **electoral votes** to win.

The next day, Gore **conceded** the election to Bush. Gore had won more popular votes than Bush. But Bush had won more electoral votes. So on January 20, 2001, George W. Bush became the forty-third president. He had won one of America's most historic elections.

Opposite page: Bush makes his election victory speech on December 13, 2000.

Glossary

alcohol - a colorless liquid found in beer, whiskey, and wine.

appeal - to bring a case to a higher court to be heard again.

ballot - a piece of paper used to cast a vote.

board of directors - a group of people that manages something, such as a company or a school district.

cancer - a disease caused by abnormal cell growth.

ceremony - a special act to be done on special occasions.

concede - to admit that something is true. In an election, the candidate who concedes is admitting defeat.

Congress - the lawmaking body of the U.S. It is made up of the Senate and the House of Representatives. It meets in Washington, D.C.

consultant - a person who gives business advice.

corporate welfare - anything a government gives to a corporation, such as free land, low-interest loans, or tax breaks, that is not given to others.

county - one of the districts into which a state is divided.

electoral votes - the votes cast by the electoral college. The electoral college is a group that elects the president and vice president. When people vote for president, the political party that gets the most votes in each state sends its representatives to the electoral college. There, they vote for their party's candidate.

fraternity - a club of men at a college.

industry - a particular branch of business, trade, or manufacturing.

invest - to use money to buy something that will produce a profit.

juvenile - of or relating to boys and girls.

lease - a written agreement for the use of property for a fixed amount of time.

literacy - the ability to read and write.

nominate - to name a candidate for office.

reform - to improve by removing faults.

Republican - a member of a political party that is conservative and believes in small government.

second lieutenant - a military rank above master sergeant and below first lieutenant.

Senate - the upper house in the U.S. Congress. Citizens elect senators to make laws for the nation.

Social Security - a government program to give money to sick, injured, or retired people and their families.

Supreme Court - the highest, most powerful court in the U.S.

Vietnam War - a long, failed attempt by the U.S. from 1955 to 1975 to help keep North Vietnam from taking over South Vietnam.

welfare - aid that the government gives to people in need.

Internet Sites

The Presidents of the United States of America
http://www.whitehouse.gov/WH/glimpse/presidents.html
This site is from the White House.

Republican National Committee
http://www.rnc.org
This is the official Web site of the Republican National Committee. Find information about the 2000 election and George W. Bush here.

These sites are subject to change. Go to your favorite search engine and type in United States Presidents for more sites.

Index